REMARKABLE CONVERSIONS,

INTERESTING INCIDENTS AND

STRIKING ILLUSTRATIONS

BY

HENRY CLAY MORRISON

First Fruits Press
Wilmore, Kentucky
c2013

ISBN: 9781621711216 (Print), 9781621711223 (Digital)

Remarkable Conversions, Interesting Incidents and Striking Illustrations by
Henry Clay Morrison
First Fruits Press, © 2013
Pentecostal Publishing Company, ©1925

Digital version at
http://place.asburyseminary.edu/firstfruitsheritagematerial/26/

Morrison, H. C. (Henry Clay), 1857-1942.
    Remarkable conversions, interesting incidents and striking illustrations
/ by Henry Clay Morrison.
    125 p. ; 21 cm.
    Wilmore, Ky. : First Fruits Press, c2013.
    Reprint. Previously published: Louisville, Ky. : Herald Press, c1925.
    ISBN: 9781621711216 (pbk.)
    1. Pastoral theology -- Anecdotes, facetiae, satire, etc. 2. Conversion --
    Anecdotes, facetiae, satire, etc. 3. Conversion -- Anecdotes. I. Title.
BV4014 .M6 2013   253

Cover design by Haley Hill

asburyseminary.edu
800.2ASBURY
204 North Lexington Avenue
Wilmore, Kentucky 40390

First Fruits
THE ACADEMIC OPEN PRESS OF ASBURY SEMINARY

Remarkable Conversions
Interesting Incidents
and
Striking Illustrations

by Dr. H. C. Morrison

Remarkable Conversions, Interesting Incidents and Striking Illustrations

By
REV. H. C. MORRISON, D.D.

HERALD PRESS
LOUISVILLE, KENTUCKY

DEDICATION

This book is affectionately dedicated to any and all persons who may have received any benefit from my ministry, hoping that its contents may stimulate a larger faith in, and a deeper and holier love for our blessed Lord and Savior Jesus Christ.

PREFACE

Many of my friends have asked me from time to time to write down much of the matter contained in this volume. I have selected a few outstanding conversions and some of the interesting incidents of a ministry of almost half a century in many lands. It has been a pleasure to me to refresh my memory and look back to the blessings that have come to us from God on many occasions in a very gracious way. Many remarkable conversions crowd my mind, and many incidents that I had not thought of for years, come up before me. I have selected these few with the hope that they may prove interesting and helpful to those who may read them.

H. C. MORRISON

CONTENTS

CHAPTER I.

ONE OF THE MOST REMARKABLE CONVER-SIONS UNDER MY MINISTRY

He was a man of about seventy years of age. In his younger days, he was a blacksmith by trade. For awhile, he was a sailor. He was a cavalry soldier in the United States Army during the Civil War. When there was no enemy to fight, he fought his comrades and spent no little time in the Guardhouse. At the close of the War, he came back to Kentucky and lived in the town where I found him.

When I discovered him, he lived in the basement of a poor shack, perched on a hillside in the suburbs of the city and made a scant living fishing and catching driftwood when the river rose and brought logs and trash from the country above. He and his wife lived alone. She was a tall, gaunt woman and knew all about an abusive husband and hard times.

Sam is what we shall call him. He was often drunk and had many conflicts with the police. He had been shot up frequently and much of the time was in the workhouse of the city. The police regarded him as one of the most dangerous men in the city and when they found him drunk, took pains to get any fighting equipment he might have about him off of him before they awoke him. He served one term in the penitentiary for killing a man. He served another term for appropriating property to which he could prove no legal title. He was very profane, shrewd, and wicked. He was fearless; he understood men remarkably well, and with proper religious training and education he would have made a very remarkable man.

Passing by the cave-like shack in which he lived, I noticed his wife peering around the corner, had a badly bruised face. On inquiry, I found that Sam, in a fit of drunken anger, had beaten her severely. The police informed me that he was in the workhouse and I went out to see him. I must confess that my visit to him was more in the line of duty than of pleasure. I felt that I should see and have a talk with him, however degraded he might be or how unwilling to converse with a preacher.

When I got out to the workhouse a negro girl, who was assisting in keeping the place, let me into his cell, locked the door and went away with the key. I found myself alone with one of the most desperate men I have ever met. In my imagination, I saw my obituary in the afternoon paper. It read about like this:

"Rev. H. C. Morrison, with more zeal than wisdom, permitted himself to be locked up in a cell out at the workhouse with old Sam Mc. The man, enraged at the presence of the preacher beat him to death with a stool. It was a most unfortunate tragedy. Mr. Morrison was a promising young minister and highly respected by his many friends in this city. His presence among the people will be greatly missed. Funeral services will take place tomorrow afternoon at three o'clock in the Methodist Church."

This funeral notice looked very unpleasant to me and I determined to postpone the obsequies to some later date if possible. So, looking the man in the face as pleasantly as I could, I said, "My friend, I have come out to have a quiet talk with you and see if we (putting the emphasis on "we") cannot arrange to do a little better than we have been doing."

I extended my hand. The old man seized it and broke into tears, saying, "Mr., if anything can be done for me, it is time it was done. I am one of the most wicked men in the world."

We had a long talk together. He wept and I prayed and I felt greatly encouraged. I realized that I had met with a very unusual man. He talked with frankness and intelligence. He poured out a confession of his many sins and begged me to help him. He promised me faithfully that he would never touch another drop of liquor. I met him soon after he was released from the workhouse and found him staggering drunk. I took him by the hand and said, "Sam, you promised me that you would never take another drop of liquor." He pulled away from me, braced his feet the best he could and commenced shoving up his sleeves, saying, "I made you no such promise and don't you say I did." He said, "I promised you I would never get drunk again, but I never said I would not take my dram. I gotta have my toddy." I looked up at the clouds and said, "I believe we are going to have rain." He quieted down. We had a chat and renewed our friendship.

Soon afterward, we had a revival at our church. A certain evangelist and his wife were with us. The wife frequently did the preaching and did it well. She attracted the crowd and my old friend, Sam, slipped in one night, sat on a back seat and heard her. I suppose it was the first time he had entered the church in many years. The next night sometime before preaching I went down in the slums to preach on the street. As I went down, I met Sam, hurrying to the church. He exclaimed to me that he was going early to get a seat close to the front, so he could hear the woman preach. He said it was wonderful the way she talked. When I got back from my street service, the church was packed. Sam was sitting on the end of the third pew from the front. He was in his shirt sleeves and carried an immense walking stick. I went around, gave him a keen slap on the shoulder and putting my lips close to his ear, said, "Sam, I believe you'll get religion tonight." It surprised him greatly. I hastened away without any argument or giving him time to offer any objection to my prophecy.

At the close of the sermon he came at once to the altar. He wept and prayed most earnestly. We stayed with him until late. He went away in great grief. The next morning early, he rang the parsonage door bell. As I went down the hall, looking through the glass door, I recognized his ragged clothing and said to myself, "Sam has been converted and has come early to tell the good news." When I opened the door, I found his eyes red and his face swollen with weeping. I asked him if he had found salvation. He said, "No, but I'm still seeking, but Tom Averill is dying and something must be done for him quickly. I have come for you to go to see him. He has lived like I have. He's a wicked man. He's lost. If you can help him, you must come quickly."

I got my hat and hurried away with Sam. We warmed up to each other. I had a feeling as we hurried up the alley of the slums that there was a third person with us who was not visible to the passers-by. We went into a miserable hut and found an old raw-boned man in his seventies with his feet slipping over the brink. Sam said to him, "Tom, here's the feller who was a tellin' me that Jesus could save the likes of us. Let him talk ter you."

At a time like this, a preacher does long for divine guidance. I knelt by the old man's bedside and told him that God so loved the world that He gave His Son to die for it; that Jesus came to seek and to save the lost; that those who came to Him He would not turn away; that in His death He made an atonement for the sins of all men. I did my best to give him the very essence of the Gospel. He seemed to take it eagerly; then I prayed. I called on Sam to pray. He started out by saying, "Lord, You know I'm not fittin' to pray for anybody." We had a heart-melting time. I believe poor old Tom was saved. I earnestly hope so. It would be an unutterable joy to meet him on the other side.

Sam and I walked slowly away together, and I could feel that he was gaining ground. Meanwhile, it was very clear that we were falling deeply in love with one another. He was hanging to me for help and I was hanging to Jesus to help us both. Meanwhile, we were getting into a very blessed atmosphere of repentance and prayer and faith.

Sam came to church that night early, got close to the front and came to the altar at the first call; others came, and souls were converted. Sam hung on. He prayed aloud. Most of the congregation left. Not over ten or twelve persons remained in the church. Among them, one of the most prominent women in the city, strongly tinctured with worldliness, giving but little evidence of spiritual life, also a brilliant young doctor, a confirmed skeptic whose wife was a member of our congregation. He attended church and we were good friends. He watched the struggling penitent with great interest. It was near eleven o'clock at night when Sam arose in triumph and flung the sleeves of his ragged coat around my neck. He had the victory. He wept, he shouted, he laughed. The intellectual, worldly woman came up in tears and said, "The Lord is in this place." The young skeptical doctor seized my hand and said, "Brother Morrison, I have known old Sam Mc. since I was a boy. He has been a miserable drunkard, a poor thief. If he holds out, I will never utter another word against the Bible or the church or the saving power of Jesus Christ."

Sam did not know his age. He did not know a letter in the books. He must have been about seventy years of age. He was quite bald-headed with a little rim of dirty, straggling hair around the lower part of his head. Everybody in the church seemed to fall in love with him; he was the "Uncle Sam" of the whole congregation. The people bought him clothing, sent food up to his house. We soon got his wife down to the church and she was happily converted, and both joined the church. We made Sam sexton. He didn't know very well how to keep the building clean, but the dear, good women would slip in and do some extra work without a word of objection to him or letting him know that he was not keeping the church in the best of order. About a year after his conversion, I left the place. He held on faithfully. The pastor who succeeded me said there had not been a more miraculous conversion in all the annals of missionary work.

A good many years passed. I held a woods meeting in a community twelve miles from the little city in which Sam lived. He walked down, gave a good testimony. He heard the people witnessing to full salvation. He listened with wonder and delight. He stood up and said, "If there's any more than what I've got, I must have it. What the Lord gave me is so good I want all He's got for me." He came to the altar and entered with great humility, and, at the same time, with great boldness, into the fulness of the blessing of the Gospel of Christ. He shouted and rejoiced wonderfully. He walked back home to tell his wife of what a marvelous blessing had been poured out in his soul. He had been a great tobacco user. A few days after this gracious baptism, he came to me and said, "Do you know a man can't chaw 'baccer and have this blessin'? I took one chaw after I got this and the Master rebuked me. I ain't a-goin' to chaw no more. I don't want no more."

Not long afterward, there was a big rise in the river. His fishing boat and tackle were all washed away. He walked seventy miles down to Louisville, came into my office, laughing and rejoicing and said, "My boat and fishin' tackle is all gone and I jis' come down here to live with you. I'll take charge of this buildin', build your fires and sweep your floors."

I consented, and we rented him a house. He sent for his wife and was with us several years. He was a blessing to the place. Everybody loved him. I frequently went up to his house for prayer. I do not believe that any human being ever loved me with a warmer, more loyal heart than "Uncle Sam."

One Saturday evening, Mr. Pritchard paid him his weekly wages and he left the office praising God. He went home, threw the money into his wife's lap, gave God glory, left the house and undertook to cross the street on some mission. He had grown quite deaf and was now very old, I should think at least eighty years of age. He stepped in front of a swiftly moving street car which lifted him high into the air. It seemed that he was dead when he fell back upon the pavement. I judge his soul was in Heaven before his dear old body struck the cobblestones.

I was preaching at the Wichita camp meeting. Mr. Pritchard sent me a telegram, telling me of "Uncle Sam's" death. Of course, it gave me grief, but I went off into the woods by myself, except my invisible Friend, and wept and laughed and shouted quietly the praises of our Saviour, and felt fully assured that my dear old friend had landed safely in eternal blessedness at the feet of that glorious Christ who is able to save to the uttermost.

It is simply wonderful how far Christ can reach with His loving arms after the fallen, and how omnipotent His majestic shoulders to bring back the lost to pardon and purity and peace and everlasting life and blessedness.

CHAPTER II

THE MAN WITH SNAKES IN HIS BOOTS AND MONKEYS ON HIS BEDPOST

I had been called to assist in a revival in a beautiful little city up in Virginia. The pastor of the Methodist Church was a most delightful Christian gentleman. If I should mention his name, it would be like ointment poured forth and known throughout the borders of Southern Methodism, and, in many places, around the world. Since then, he has been a very successful and much beloved missionary.

Soon after the beginning of the meeting, my attention was called to a young man in the town, the son of an excellent family who had been successful in business, but had taken to drink. He had gone from bad to worse, his business had failed, a good property had been swept away. At the present time, he was having delirium tremens. Some young men were laboring with him very faithfully. They would take him into the woods, on a creek bank, during the day and keep him there,—a fine thing

by the way; the deep, silent woods, on the bank
of a clear, gurgling creek, is a place for calm
thought and earnest prayer,—a good place for
a struggling soul to seek after God. These young
friends would bring their fighting victim into
church at night and sit with him on the back
seat. As the days went forward, he improved a
bit. He became less violent. He gradually so-
bered. On the last night of the meeting, they
brought him to the altar and he was happily
converted. It was a wonderful transformation.

Before his conversion, I had gone up to his
cottage to talk and pray with him. His yard
gate was off the hinges and his yard rooted up
by the pigs. Weatherboarding had been torn
off his cottage and it was in great need of re-
pairs and paint. In the house, there were broken
chairs and a little dilapidated furniture. His
wife, lean and gaunt, in faded dress, sat on a
piece of chair with her head down. A little
baby sat on the floor with a hard crust in its
hand and a swarm of flies about its face. It
was a wretched place. The whiskey demon, it
seemed, had done his worst.

Some three months afterward, I spent a few

days in the same town. I met the pastor in front of his church and after a cordial greeting, he insisted that I should preach in the church on Wednesday evening, which I promised to do. He then said, "Step across the street to that grocery; there is a man there who would like to see you." I went over. A big, handsome, well dressed man rushed from behind the counter, grabbed my hand and squeezed it until the bones ached. He expressed his great joy at seeing me. I confessed that I did not know him. "Why," said he, "I am the fellow that had the snakes in my boots and the monkeys on my bedposts when you were here in your revival meeting. Don't you remember I was converted the last night of the meeting." I did remember at once and we rejoiced together. He said, "I have not had the slightest appetite or desire for whiskey from that night to this time." He said, "You must take supper with me Thursday evening. My wife will be delighted to see you." I was glad to accept his invitation. After preaching in the church on Wednesday evening, many friends came up to greet me, among them a beautiful woman, tastefully dressed, with roses in her cheeks, laughter in her mouth, and tears in her eyes. She said, "I want you to take sup-

per with us Thursday evening." I thanked her,
but said to her, "I promised to take supper
with my friend, Frank," naming this remarkable convert. She answered in laughter, "I am
Frank's wife." I was greatly surprised and a
bit displeased. I hardly thought it the proper
thing for this new convert to bury the poor
wretched looking creature of a wife he had just
three months ago and marry this beautiful young
woman in so short a time. But on inquiry, I
found it was the same woman. The difference
was when I saw her the first time, she was the
wife of a miserable lost drunkard, jabbering about
with delirium tremens. When I saw her three
months later, she was the wife of a wonderfully
saved man, filled with the joy of the Lord,
prosperous and happy in his business.

You may be sure I went up to their house
for supper the next evening. The gate was on
its hinges, the fence had been repaired, the yard
was in good order, the cottage had been mended
and painted white as snow. When I entered
the house, there was a carpet on the floor, well-
arranged furniture, books on the shelves and
pictures on the wall. When supper came, there
was T-bone steak in plenty and a fat rosy-cheek

baby sitting in a high chair without a fly on him. I was profoundly impressed. I renewed my faith and purpose to preach a Christ who is so mighty and so gracious to save.

Back yonder three months ago, at a late hour in the evening, at the altar of the Methodist Church, there had been a new birth. It was the beginning of a new life. Old things had passed away; all things had become new. This new birth and new life is a powerful and irrefutable evidence of the Godhead and saving power of the Lord Jesus. This is an argument that cannot be answered.

Shortly after this visit to old Virginia, I met with one of the distinguished lawyers of old Kentucky, a friend of mine, who was an infidel. We got into a discussion about the inspiration of the Scriptures, the deity of Christ and His power to save sinners. When I got opportunity I related to him the above incident and he became deeply interested. At the close, I said, "Colonel, all skepticism in all the world has never taken the snakes out of a man's boots, the monkeys off his bedposts, put into him the power of a new life, planted roses in the cheeks of his wife and frightened the flies off of his baby." I said, "Colonel, if I have a lie and you have the truth, my falsehood is worth a million times more to the human race in its sorrow and sin than your truth, for this Gospel that I preach is winning multitudes of lost sinners to Christ, to pardon and peace, to salvation and victory, to happy hearts and joyful homes, while your infidelity is only destroying faith, blighting hope and sending sinners adrift into darkness." I said, "Colonel, I have the truth and you have the falsehood."

He said, "Brother Morrison, if I believed the Bible as you believe it and could preach what you claim to be the Gospel with the faith and joy that you have, I would rather preach the Gospel than to be President of the United States." We took a long walk together. He was one of the handsomest and most eloquent men I ever saw or heard. I said, "Colonel, I love you. You have a great soul, but you are in error and you are in darkness. I am going to pray for you and I hope, through the mercy of God, that sometime in the future, somewhere in the grand galleries of God's universe, I may meet you graciously saved and rejoicing in Jesus."

The great lawyer wept, he pressed my hand and said, "I want you to pray for me." Soon afterward, he died, and in his dying hour, he cried aloud and most earnestly to God for mercy. Who knows but the Christ, whose mighty arms of mercy caught the thief away from the cross to Paradise, may have reached out in answer to prayer and caught this poor man away from the verge of the pit to eternal blessedness?

CHAPTER III

A GRACIOUS MANIFESTATION OF GRACE

Some twenty or twenty-five years ago, I was assisting in a revival meeting in one of our great Eastern cities. The Lord was blessing us and quite a number of people were professing salvation at the altar of prayer. An unusually handsome young man came to the altar at almost every service. He manifested no emotion, shed no tears and did not seem to be in prayer. He would bow his head at the altar rail and when anyone rose up blessed he would lift up his head and look at them calmly, and then bow again to lift up his head when anyone was rejoicing and gaze about among the happy people for sometime, with a very blank, peculiar expression.

One evening after service, he asked if he might walk with me to my boarding place. I willingly consented. As we walked along the street, he unburdened his heart; he told me that he was not quite twenty-four years of age, but that he felt he had completely sinned away his day of grace and that there was no help or hope for him; that he had been coming to the altar simply on the advice of some friends who thought it might possibly warm up his heart and make repentance possible.

He told me of his sins. He had blighted a life; he had sworn a lie, he had signed a false statement and while he had not actually committed murder, he had been connected with the planning of a murder and felt that he was as wicked as if he had committed murder with his own hand. I have hardly ever heard just such a confession as he made. He said that for a number of years he had not been able to pray, that he could feel no emotion, that he could shed no tears, that while he regretted his wickedness and would give the world, if he owned it, to undo his past, yet there seemed to be a cold deadness in his heart and that he was not conscious of any godly sorrow; that for several years he had walked about with a sort of graveyard in his breast, in which everything that was good or could produce happiness, repentance for sins or exercise faith seemed to be dead and buried. He asked if I thought it was at all worthwhile for him to go to the altar or if I could believe there was any mercy for so great sinner as he had been.

We had just come under a street light. I wheeled suddenly around, caught him by the lapel of his coat, gave him a vigorous shake and said, "Doesn't the Bible say that Jesus Christ came to seek and save the lost?" And then crying out as loud as I dared on the street, I said, "Aren't you lost? No doubt Jesus is seeking you!" He looked at me with surprise and then broke into tears. As we walked toward my boarding house he said, "Well, thank God, I have some feeling and these are the first tears I have shed for several years. I wouldn't take the world for these tears. It may be that there is mercy for me."

I stopped at my doorstep and we talked for sometime. I urged him to press on, to let nothing prevent him seeking the Lord on all public occasions, and constantly in private, and to remind himself that Jesus had come "to seek and save the lost."

As we parted, he expressed great gratitude for the good words of encouragement and said again and again, "I am so thankful that I can weep, that that awful hardness is broken up; there must be hope for me." I saw nothing more of the young man, and often wondered what had become of him.

This fall, while preaching in one of the Eastern cities, frequently at the night services I noticed back in the congregation a large, well-dressed, handsome gentleman. He gave the closest attention and had a most receptive face and I judged from his appearance and manifestation that he was a devout Christian. On the last night of the meeting, he came forward and gave me a most hearty and brotherly greeting and assured me that he had attended the services as frequently as possible and had been greatly benefited by the meeting. He held on to my hand and looking up with a beaming countenance, he said, "We have met before. Do you recall a good many years ago a young man walked home with you when you were holding revival meetings in a certain city and told you of his great wickedness and that for several years he had felt that there was no hope for him; that he had sinned away his day of grace; that he couldn't feel any contrition or pray with any faith, and that you insisted to the young man that he was lost and that Jesus had come to seek and to save the lost?"

The incident flashed into my mind at once and I assured that I did remember very distinctly the whole matter as he related it.

"Well," said he, "I am the man." He said, "I sought the Lord and found Him most graciously. He called me into the ministry and for a number of years I have been preaching the blessed Gospel and the Lord has sealed my ministry in the salvation of many precious souls." We rejoiced together for a few moments; friends were crowding about to bid me goodbye and we had no time for further conversation.

The reader may be sure that I was delighted to meet this man and to hear the witness from his lips of the wonderful mercy of God and the gracious power of Jesus to save from sin.

Relating this incident reminds me that quite frequently in my ministry and by correspondence I have met up with or come in touch with persons who believed they had committed unpardonable sin and for them there was no hope and, in a number of instances, I have been able to help them back to repentance and saving faith. I recall one case of a young man who had brooded over his sins and his lost condition until he had been sent to a sanitarium for the insane. He wrote to me from that place. We had quite a correspondence. He was finally able to exercise saving faith in Jesus. His heart was comforted with peace, his health improved, his mental equilibrium was restored and the last time I heard from him he was preaching the Gospel.

I think a very large number of people at sometime in life are more or less troubled with the fear that they had sinned away their day of grace and that for them there is no mercy or hope. In fact, this is one of Satan's shrewd schemes. First, he will say to the sinner, "There is no danger; God is merciful. Enjoy yourself. Gratify your appetites. Feed your passion. Get the most out of life. There is plenty of time." And thus he will draw the soul away from God into sin. Second, he will turn upon the soul and say, "You have gone too far. There is no hope. You can't repent. God will not be merciful. He has entirely cast you away and it is useless to seek salvation." This father of lies has no truth in him. He is lying when he says there is no danger and he is also lying when he says there is no hope. There is great danger in sin, in any sin, of any character; there is great danger in delay, but there is hope; repentance is possible and God delights in mercy, however far the prodigal may have wandered; however fallen and fearful may be his or her condition. When the lost soul turns to God, pleading the name of Jesus, there is mercy. If any one should read these lines who has fallen into despair, do not listen longer to the voice of the tempter, but throw yourself upon the divine mercy of God, plead with Him, cling to Him, tell Him how that the Christ who has tasted death for every man has tasted death for you, and let no one, man or devil, persuade you that you may not repent and pray and trust in Jesus Christ for salvation.

CHAPTER IV

THE DIFFERENCE IN OFFERING PRAYER AND ISSUING ORDERS

Something more than thirty years ago I was assisting the pastor of King Avenue Church, Columbus, Ohio, in revival meetings. At that time only the Sunday school room of that splendid structure had been erected. I was entertained in the home of a very pleasant family, and one afternoon was called down to the parlor to meet a young woman who had been attending the services and was in great distress. She was elegantly dressed and had the appearance of education and refinement.

She said, "Mr. Morrison, I have been attending your meetings and I am in great trouble over my spiritual state and thought I would call and have a talk with you. I have been a member of the church from my childhood and have tried to live a consistent life. I have never asked God for very much, but for four years I have been praying earnestly about one thing, and it does not seem that I can get an answer.

If God does not answer this prayer I will lose all faith and become a confirmed skeptic. I am distressed beyond words to express. It does seem that I ought to have an answer to this one prayer, and after praying so long and so earnestly, if this request is refused how can I have faith and pray with any expectation of being heard in other matters? If the Lord does not answer this prayer I shall never pray again."

I said, "My dear friend, that is not offering prayer to God at all; it is issuing orders to him; it is telling Him that you want Him to do certain things, that if He will do those things you will continue to ask for His favors and send up petitions to Him; and if He does not you will never speak to Him again. There is a wide difference, my friend, between a humble, earnest prayer to God and the issuing of orders to Him, with a threat attached that, if He should not obey your orders there cannot be any further communion or fellowship between you and Him."

She insisted that I misunderstood her, but I insisted that her prayers were in the spirit of a dictation rather than a humble petition.

We were both in tears: she was weeping bitterly, my heart was deeply moved with pity, but I felt it was not worth-while to pray until her attitude toward God was changed. We sat in silence for sometime, meanwhile, I was wondering what it was about which she had been praying so long and so earnestly. By and by, a thought struck me and at a venture I said, "Sister, it is quite probable if you should marry the young man you have been praying over, and asking God for so earnestly for this long time, he would turn out to be a curse rather than a blessing. He might whip you and leave you in less than a year."

She broke out weeping aloud, and said, "How did you know that was it?" I answered, "I did not know but now I see the situation very clearly. You love some young man far better than you love God. You would put Jesus off of the throne of your heart and place this young man on the throne. You are making your beloved first, and the Lord second. You are seeking to make a servant out of the Lord, to have Him do various and sundry odd jobs for you in order that you may have enough confidence in Him and respect for Him to give Him other things to do. This is not prayer at all; true prayer recognizes the supremacy of God; it makes him Lord of all. It is always in the spirit of 'not my will, but thine be done.' It recognizes the ignorance and shortsightedness of ourselves and the infinite wisdom and mercy of God who knows far better than we what is best for us."

She dried her tears, became quiet and thoughtful, and we had quite a conversation on the weakness and mistakes of the human, of how we might approach the throne of God in the spirit of masters instead of servants; of selfishness instead of love; that it was possible to seek to use God instead of being used of Him.

She admitted her mistake, became very humble and agreed that she was not in a converted state at all, but simply a church member trying to live respectably, render some little service to the church, and use God to bring about the consummation of her selfish wishes. She promised me to seek her soul's salvation; to lay other things aside and get right with Jesus.

We prayed together and she left me seeming to have lost interest in the young man and promising to seek the Lord until she found Him. She attended the evening service, and at the conclusion of the sermon, came to the altar, was a most earnest seeker and was very happily converted.

I had no further conversation with her, but judge from her appearance that she largely lost interest in the young man with whom she had been so desperately in love. As I thought on the matter I could but believe it would be better for many persons to settle their love affairs at an altar of prayer and crown Jesus Lord of all.

Thinking over this experience I am reminded that the same night in which this young lady was converted, I went into the audience and spoke to a number of persons about their spiritual state. I remember distinctly that one young man answered that he was unsaved, and that his condition was hopeless. We conversed some time together. He said that he had been educated at Ohio Wesleyan University, and during his time in the University he had been converted and called to the ministry. Prior to this time he had his heart set on the law; he had very lofty ambitions; that he was so unwilling to give up these ambitions and preach that, in order to get rid of the strong impression that the Holy Spirit had made upon him to preach, he had neglected the means of grace, was encouraged to become worldly-minded and had grieved away the Holy Spirit; that for some four years he had been in utter darkness, that he had ceased to pray, that he had no hope for the salvation of his soul; that he would willingly go to the altar of prayer if he thought it would do him any good, but he was confident there was no help or hope for him, and that it would be quite useless for him to try to pray or for anyone else to pray for him.

I prevailed upon him, however, to go forward for prayer. He fell down at the altar a picture of utter despair; he remained there while a number were saved: the meeting continued until late in the evening, and when he arose there was a sign of moisture in his eyes, he gripped my hand and thanked me for inducing him to come to the altar and said to me, "I have made up my mind that if I go to hell I will go there praying. I intend to give myself to this one thing of seeking my soul's salvation, and if I am lost at last I will be lost calling on God for mercy."

I assured him that I felt his situation was most hopeful. The next evening we had some testimonies before the sermon. I had stood up in the pulpit and was just about to announce my text when this young man came into the audience. His head was lifted up and his face was shining. I saw at once that he had found the Lord, and said, "Perhaps there is some one else who would like to give a testimony before I read my text."

He spoke out joyfully and said, "You will recall our conversation last night. You will remember that I was at the altar and told you I would seek until I found mercy or died calling on Christ for help. Last night at two o'clock at my bedside, Jesus came back to me, took all my sins away and graciously blessed my soul."

He was very happy indeed. He had come up out of the darkness of despair into the marvelous light of salvation. I regret that I failed to get his name and to keep track of his subsequent history. I trust that he went into the ministry and was graciously used of the Lord. I think, however, it is possible for one in his condition to be reclaimed and not to be honored with a recall into the ministry. I well remember when I was assisting Dr. Sam Steel in meetings in old McKendree Church, Nashville, Tenn., one of the young women teachers in Dr. Price's female college, was a seeker at the altar. She told me when she had been converted some years ago she was called to the mission field, that she refused to answer the call, and that she backslid. She was very penitent, eager to be saved, and anxious to become a missionary. During the meetings she was graciously reclaimed but told me in great sorrow, sometime afterward, that her call to the mission field had not come back, and she felt that by refusing to obey the Lord when she was first converted, that while He had mercifully saved her, He was not going to honor her by sending her out to win heathen souls to Christ. Disobedience to the call of God is fraught with great danger.

CHAPTER V

RESTORATION AND SALVATION

On my first trip across the continent, going out to California to hold several revivals, I had arranged to stop and help Rev. T. L. Adams in a meeting in a little city in the mountains of New Mexico. I got into El Paso, Texas, Saturday afternoon and finding that I could not get to Brother Adams until Sabbath morning I determined to remain in El Paso until Monday. I have made it a rule through my evangelistic life, not to travel on the Sabbath. I found a comfortable hotel at a moderate price and comforted myself with the thought that I would get some needed rest. I retired early Saturday evening, and directly after lying down a voice seemed to speak within me as clear to my consciousness as if it had been audible, telling me that I must preach in El Paso. I was quite surprised as I did not know a soul in El Paso, and had never been in that region before. I got out of bed at once and prayed for divine guidance. When I got back into bed the voice

43

spoke again, assuring me that I must preach in El Paso. I got up and prayed the second time. I could not understand how I could possibly preach in that city as I was a perfect stranger and could see no possibility of remaining there to preach. When I got back into bed the same command to preach in El Paso was repeated. I hurried and got upon my knees with a very gracious consciousness of the divine presence, and breaking into laughter I said, "Lord, if thou wilt open the door I will enter it." I got back to bed with a very sweet assurance that the door would be opened. I had a good night's rest, awoke early, took my bath, dressed, and went for a walk before breakfast. I inquired of some one where the Methodist Church was located, went down, looked the church over and supposed it would be the place of the open door.

After breakfast when time came for Sunday school, I went to the church and on entering the auditorium, was met by an unusually impressive woman who walked up and, shaking hands with me said, "You must be a stranger in our city?" I replied that I was. She asked from what state I came and I told her Kentucky. She said, "I am from Kentucky; was born and raised in Maysville." I told her that I had held two revival meetings in Maysville. I called the names of a number of persons she knew. She seemed greatly pleased to meet with me and said, "I must introduce you to the pastor," which she did. He had never heard of me before but finding that I was a Methodist minister insisted that I should preach for him at the 11 o'clock hour. I refused, but consented to preach in the evening. He announced that I would preach at the evening service, and asked the people to come and bring their friends. We had a large and deeply interested audience. The Lord gave me liberty and we had a good time.

Before dismissing, the pastor said to me, "I am beginning a protracted meeting today, and you certainly came here in the providence of God, and must stay and preach for me." I said to him that he might announce me for Monday evening, but that he must come to the hotel the next morning and let us talk over the matter of the meeting.

When he came to the hotel next morning I gave him a bit of my history, told him that I stood for the Wesleyan interpretation of the doctrine of holiness, and that I claimed the experience of full salvation, that I preached entire sanctification as a second work of grace, and in revival meetings called Christians to the altar to seek the experience. Tears came into the man's eyes and he said, "My brother, I am seeking for that grace and will welcome you most heartily to preach full redemption to my people." I wrote Brother Adams explaining my delay and went to work for a two weeks' revival in El Paso.

This has been some thirty or more years ago; El Paso was a small city, compared to what it is at present. The M. E. Church, South, was a small wooden structure with a comparatively small membership. The Lord was very gracious to us, there being a number of souls converted, but the great feature of the meeting was the number of persons definitely sanctified, among them the pastor and his wife; also the very excellent woman who greeted me at the door on Sunday morning as I entered the church, Mrs. Lydia Patterson. Mrs. Corbin, the wife of Rev. Corbin who has been so long connected with mission work in Mexico, one of the finest Christian women I have ever known, came into the experience. The pastor and his wife in our Mexican church, with several other fine Mexican people were graciously baptized with the Holy Spirit in sanctifying power.

Mrs. Patterson, who was the wife of a prominent and wealthy lawyer of the city, became a most remarkable and influential Christian character in that growing western city. She was known and loved very generally among the people of all the churches, and those outside, for her beautiful Christian character and her many good works. She had a broad and abiding influence for Christ and His great salvation. It was through this influence that the large Mexican mission school was built in El Paso, her husband giving a handsome sum of money for its erection. The school bears her name, "The Lydia Patterson Institute," and for many years has been doing a great work among the Mexican people.

This, however, is not the story I had in mind when sitting down to write of "Restoration and Salvation." I went, at the close of this meeting to assist my good brother, T. L. Adams. I found him living in a little one-room adobe hut, cooking, eating, sleeping, studying and praying all in the same room. T. L. Adams, now in his old age, in the city of Los Angeles, is one of the most humble, sweet-spirited, prayerful, faithful, Christian men I have ever known. To me, he seems to be in all things blameless.

Brother Adams was living in a mining town, a desperately wicked place. I well remember that the butcher rode behind his meat delivery wagon with a Winchester in his lap, to keep men from robbing his delivery boy. There were a number of mines and villages of little shacks all about the place. A large Indian town was near, and the streets were filled with a mixed multitude of miners, cowboys, Mexicans, Indians, and all sorts of foreigners who had drifted into this mining region.

Brother Adams and I had a gracious time of prayer, wrestling and rejoicing in the little adobe hut. The Holy Spirit was with us most graciously; the memory of those days refreshes my soul. The revival broke out, conviction was deep; a few were wholly sanctified and quite a number were converted. We gathered a little group of godly men and women together and went all over the town praying in the homes of the people. I think we entered every house, shack and shed where anybody lived, and had prayer. These prayer meetings in the homes of the people had a wonderful effect; in almost every home they broke down, wept, and thanked us for coming, and in a number of instances, the people in these homes attended the meetings and were blessedly saved.

One Sunday afternoon Brother Adams and I were going over the mountain to a mining village to hold an afternoon service. A young man living in the town where we were holding the meeting, galloped up behind us and asked Brother Adams to ride his horse and let him walk with me. Brother Adams mounted his horse and the young man and myself, leaving the main road, took an Indian trail up among the big rocks on a short cut, and as we went along he told me his story.

He said, "Mr. Morrison, I have been to the altar of prayer in your meeting but I shall not come back. I have some confessions and restorations to make before I can be saved." I insisted that God would take him on credit; that if he made a sincere promise God would forgive his sins and go with him to help him make his confessions and restorations.

He said, "There are many restorations I can never make. I came from another state out here, determined to make money. My father was a poor man; our relatives about us were wealthy. The boys and girls, our cousins, went off to college. They had beautiful homes, fine clothes, but we were embarrassed with our poverty. I resolved that my sisters should be well-dressed and sent to college. I have worked hard, sent money home, and I am educating my sisters. I have gotten money every way possible without straight-out stealing. I have the largest business in this town, and I can hardly claim an honest dollar. When you came here I had on foot a dishonest scheme. I was planning to sell a worthless newspaper, which was losing money all the time, to a tenderfoot who has a large bank account. After hearing you preach I abandoned that scheme. But I have done so many things that were wrong. For instance, we had a horse race here on Thanksgiving Day; before the race came off I got the boys who were training the horses out onto a country road and told them to train the horses, make them run, and without the boys suspecting what I was up to, I had them put the horses out at their best; I saw one was far more fleet than the other, so when the race came off I knew which horse to bet on, and I won money from cowboys, miners, Mexicans, Indians, negroes, and people scattered over the country from all the adjoining towns, whom I had never seen before and never will see again. I cannot possibly make restoration to these parties."

I asked him to count up the number of people he had wronged, whom he knew, and to whom he could make restoration. He counted them up and they were a goodly number. He promised to see them all and straighten up matters at any cost. I said in addition to this, promise the Lord if opportunity should ever come to make restoration to others, you will gladly do so. He made the promise. We went to the village and I preached. He was the first man at the altar. He did not find peace, but pledged me that he would continue to seek.

After the service Brother Adams and I went back to the town where we were holding the meeting, and I was sitting in the abode hut building a fire. The door was fastened with a wooden button; some one leaped against the door, the wooden button flew off, the door flew open, and my young merchant, the penitent of whom I have spoken, leaped into the room shouting and praising God, seized me in his arms and said his sins had all been forgiven. Brother Adams came in and we had a time of rejoicing. Early the next morning he started on his round of confession and restoration. He was radiant with joy and praise.

I went to California and some four months later came back and spent eight or ten days with Brother Adams in another meeting, and found this same young man superintendent of his Sunday school, growing in grace, and with a very wide Christian influence in all the community. He was indeed in Christ a new creature. There is nothing more wonderful than that divine power found by faith in Jesus Christ that saves men from the love of their sins, and the guilt of their sins, transforms them in a moment and makes them to hate what they loved, and love what they hated; makes them in deed and in truth, new creatures in Christ.

CHAPTER VI
A FATHER'S PRAYERS ARE ANSWERED

When I was on my Evangelistic Tour of the world, Rev. J. L. Piercy, my traveling companion, and myself, landed in Bombay, India, one morning. We were met by friends and were hurried in our preparation to start for Lucknow on the afternoon train. Lucknow was the point at which the convention for which we had come was to be held.

Methodism is a great power in India; Methodist missions were planted there at a most fortunate time. The first missionaries of the Methodist Church were of the finest type, wide vision, deep piety, and strong faith. Such men as Bishop Thoburn helped to lay the foundation of the Methodist Church in India. He was followed by men of the type and spirit of Bishops Warne and Oldham. One of the most fortunate events in the history of the mission work in India was the visit and labors of Bishop William Taylor. Eternity alone can tell of the gracious

influence of his life and ministry among the
most spiritual and devout of all Methodism.

For many years it was their habit to hold a
great convention in Lucknow for the deepening
of the spiritual life of the people. They generally secured some minister of the gospel, either
from England or the United States, to preach
at this convention. It was a call to preach at
this great gathering that opened the door for
my Evangelistic Tour of the World.

I had gone into the parsonage for a little
chat with the station missionaries before en-
training for Lucknow. When I came out a
very old gentleman leaning on a staff was talking earnestly to Brother Piercy. I found on
conversation with him that he was an old British
soldier retired on pension. He was a devout
Christian, and very solicitous for the salvation
of his son, who was also a soldier, and stationed
with a certain battery in Lucknow. He turned
to me and, with much emotion said, "My son
is a fine lad. He is a good soldier, but he has
never been converted. I have been praying
very earnestly for the dear boy, and since I
heard you were coming I have been believing
for his conversion at your meetings in Luck-

now. My name is Bishop, and here is the name
of my boy, and the number of his battery. I
want you to look him up and I am trusting
the Lord to bring him to Christ during your
meeting."

We assured the old gentleman that we would
make it a point to do our best to secure his
soul's salvation. As we drove away to the depot Brother Piercy said, "That old father's
faith is wonderful. I believe the boy will be
converted." I expressed the same belief. I
said, "He is like a needle in a haystack. Lucknow is a city of 300,000 people, and there are
6,000 British troops stationed there, but we
must find young Bishop and do our utmost to
bring him to Christ."

We had a very interesting twenty-four-hours'
trip up to Lucknow, and a very gracious greeting by the host of missionaries and native people gathered for the convention. The services
were held in the chapel of the Isabella Thoburn
Girls' College. Christian College for young men
is also located at Lucknow, and we had a large
attendance of students. The first night of the
meeting, as I stood in the pulpit preaching,
my attention was attracted to a very fine look-

ing British soldier. His uniform was of immaculate whiteness, with a fine array of braid and brass buttons. His hair was black as a crow's wing, and his arms were folded on his breast, his head thrown back, and he gave closest attention.

At the close of the sermon I called for seekers of salvation, and at once a number came to the altar. I stepped over the altar rail, went down the aisle and extended my hand to the handsome soldier; he looked at me with surprise, held out his hand, and gave me a firm grip. I said, "Are you a Christian?" He answered at once, "I am not, Sir." "Well," said I, "don't you think you ought to be a Christian?" "I do, Sir," was his prompt reply. "Will you go with me to the altar and seek the forgiveness of your sins?" "I will, Sir." As he spoke he arose and we walked rapidly up the aisle together, he fell on his knees and began to pray most earnestly.

We had quite an altar service; a number claimed to be blessed, but my soldier remained upon his knees. When the service was dismissed I stepped up to him and asked, "Have you found salvation?" He answered, "I have not,

Sir." "Will you be back to the meeting tomorrow night, and if you have not found peace,
continue to seek the Lord?" He answered, "I
will, Sir." He kept his promise, next evening
was in his place and when the call was made
came at once to the altar. I knelt with him
and we fought it out together; he was graciously saved; we threw our arms about each other,
and took a long embrace of brotherhood in
Christ. We then looked into each other's faces
and I asked him, "What is your name?" "My
name is Bishop, and my father, who is a true
Christian man, is praying for me down in Bombay." "Why," said, I, "I met your father, and
I have your name and number of your battery
in my pocket." I drew the card from my vest
pocket and handed it to him. We were both
surprised and delighted. We were also very
happy in the thought that the great Father is
full of mercy and grace.

You may be sure that young Bishop and I
fell in love with each other. He was not only
a constant attendant at the meetings but
brought other soldiers with him, and was very
earnest in his prayers and solicitation for the
salvation of his comrades. I have scarcely found

finer material for evangelism than among the British soldiers in India. In several places where we held our meetings British soldiers were stationed and we were always able to gather some fine seals for the Master from among them.

During the World War I received a letter stained with muddy water, from a trench in France, written by a British soldier, who was graciously sanctified in one of our meetings in India. He told of how God was keeping him, and what a blessing The Pentecostal Herald, which had followed him to the battlefield, had been to him, in the many trials and dangers through which he had passed. He said frequently when a great shell was about to explode near him, he would leap into the trench or shell hole and close his eyes, thinking that perhaps, when he opened them again he would be looking upon his glorious Redeemer.

My touch with the British soldiers in India impressed upon me the value of the careful instruction of children in the Catechism. There is nothing quite so important in the education of a child as thorough instruction in the fundamental principles of Bible truth, and true knowledge of the steps that lead one from a state of sin to a state of salvation through faith in our Lord and Saviour Jesus Christ.

The prayer of faith will bring its reward. It was our Lord Jesus who taught us that "Men ought always to pray, and not to faint." By which he means to teach us that we ought to pray always, and never become discouraged or give up praying and believing that God will hear and answer.

CHAPTER VII

UNLOADING A COW

Many years ago I was holding revival meetings in a little town in Texas; there was in the town a very prominent young man; tall, handsome, full of courtesy and good humor. He was a clerk in the largest store in town and easily the most popular and influential young man in the little city.

He fell under deep conviction, came to the altar of prayer seeking salvation. He wept bitterly, prayed earnestly and manifested the deepest concern in his soul's salvation. He came many times to the altar; I instructed him the best I knew, and the Christians of the community seemed to take a deep interest in him, many of them talking and praying with him.

After he had been at the altar a number of times I wondered if there was not some serious difficulty in his way, and asked him why it was that he seemed so very earnest, and came so frequently to the altar; there must be something peculiar in his case. I suggested that possibly he would have to make a confession or restoration. He wept bitterly, and said there was nothing of the kind in his way. I found in this instance it was possible for a man to cry, and pray, and lie, all at the same time. I became confirmed in the opinion that either a confession or restoration was his obstacle.

He continued to come to the altar, and at the close of a morning meeting he was invited to take dinner with a group of us who were to dine with a friend. After dinner the young man asked if he could walk with me uptown, to which I readily consented. As we went along up the street he reminded me that a few days before I had asked him if confession and restoration were involved in his case. He said, "I denied at the time that any such thing was necessary, but that is my trouble." He said, "Some years ago when I was in the cattle business up in the Panhandle of Texas, I got hold of a cow that did not belong to me." (Down in Kentucky we call that stealing.) He said, "I shall never be saved until I give you the money for that cow." I explained to him that it was not my cow. "If I had only known whose cow it was," said he, "I would have sent them the money long ago. I want to give you the money for the cow and you can give it to some poor widow." I thought at once of the widow and six orphan children of one of our evangelists who had died, and told him I would have no trouble placing the cow money. He broke into tears and came very near falling in the street. I caught hold of him and with difficulty held him up until I could turn toward the fence at the side of the street, where he fell over on the ground on his face crying out, "Oh, what a relief!"

A negro boy, with two mules attached to a wagon, with four bales of cotton, himself perched on top of one of the bales, was driving just behind us. The mules frightened at my staggering, falling man, they reared and plunged, the negro boy fell backwards off his bale of cotton. I saw his heels sticking in the air, and thought to myself, I was not surprised that the mules should become frightened at a man unloading a cow off of his weary burdened conscience in the middle of the street. That cow was evidently a Texas longhorn, and she had gored the poor young man into a state of fearful desperation.

After weeping and praying for sometime by
the fence, he got slowly up. I asked him if he felt
he was saved, and he said he was not, but that
he now felt the way was open for salvation. He
went into the store where he clerked, got some
money, and we walked away together for quite
a distance, neither of us speaking. Finally, he
turned to one side and climbed a fence which
led into the forest. I followed him, and when
he had gotten some distance out in the woods,
he handed me the cow money. I put it into
my vest pocket and said, "Let us pray." We
fell on our knees, I prayed a few words and
then called on the young man. He poured out
his heart in an audible prayer. He made a most
earnest and honest confession, then pled for
mercy in the name of Jesus. Directly he was
able to exercise saving faith. He leaped and
shouted. He embraced the trees and shook hands
with the bushes. He was one of the happiest
men I ever saw.

I have not seen or heard of him for many
years. If dead, I have no doubt he is at home
in heaven; if living he is an old man and I
trust is ripe for the skies.

He never would have found peace if he had

not made his confession, and as far as possible, made restoration. There is many a poor soul that has sought salvation, but has come up to some confession or restoration that must be made, has refused to meet the conditions and has turned back into sin and darkness and eternal death.

Not long since, I was conversing with a friend of mine about a brother we had both known and loved very much; a man who had once been a very zealous Christian, but had wandered from the light. He had grown rich, and proud at heart. I asked my friend who knew this man better than I did, if there was any hope for him? He said he did not think so, and remarked that back in the early days of his fortune making, he had done certain things that involved large money matters, and that in order to be saved he would have to make humiliating confession and large financial restoration, and that the man growing rich had become such a money lover that he feared he would lose his soul rather than give up some wrongly-gotten property, in order to get right with God.

There is no man more to be pitied than that unfortunate man under bondage to the spirit of covetousness, who has come into possession of property, perhaps great wealth, unjustly, and who loves the money that does not rightly belong to him, better than he loves his soul; and will spend his eternity in hell rather than humble himself, make confession and restoration.

I was once preaching in a great city church and a prominent man in the church fell under deep conviction, and after a great battle confessed that he had arranged for the burning of his own store, and collected the insurance money, but had made up his mind to confess and make restoration to the insurance company, and if they should prosecute him, go to the penitentiary. He had found pardon and peace. He was distressed over the unfortunate situation, but said with a smile in the midst of his tears, "I would much rather spend the remainder of my time in the penitentiary than to spend all eternity in hell." Ten thousand times better to confess when necessary, and make restoration where possible, than to cover one's sin, to carry torment in one's bosom through life, and at death go into outer darkness without help or hope to all eternity.

CHAPTER VIII

AN INTERESTING INCIDENT IN MY EARLY MINISTRY

I was a beardless youth traveling the Jacksonville Circuit in the Kentucky Conference as assistant preacher to Rev. Chas. Cooper, preacher in charge. The Jacksonville Circuit embraced a part of three different counties—Shelby, Henry and Franklin. We ranged from the Kentucky River, thirteen miles below Frankfort, out onto the L. & N. Railroad up to Sweet Home near Christiansburg.

Directly after going to the Circuit, I spent the night with Rev. Peter Kavanaugh who lived in a big bend of the Kentucky River at a place known as LeCompt's Bottom. Leaving Brother Kavanaugh's early in the morning I started across the ridge for a community on Sand Riffle Creek. I had gotten some distance from the house of this most interesting and unique preacher, a nephew, by the way, of our beloved Bishop Kavanaugh. I was riding up a lane when I heard the discharge of a shotgun. Both barrels were fired so close together that it sounded almost like one report. Looking across the field, some hundreds of yards away, I saw three men running, one of them hollowing for help, with two others after him. The wounded man fell. I supposed it was a case of murder. There were several rail fences between me and the men, so I threw my bridle rein over a fence stake, dismounted and ran toward the men as rapidly as possible.

When I arrived on the scene I found that a farmer was going with his own sons over to Brother Kavanaugh's to make apple cider. One of the boys, a stout, handsome lad, some nineteen years of age, was carrying a shotgun in his hand, breech foremost. He had leaped over a ditch in the field, had stumbled and pitching forward had thrown the gun in front of him. The hammers had struck the ground, discharging both barrels. His hand had fallen upon the muzzle of the gun so that the forefinger on his right hand was shot away down to the first joint, hanging by a small bit of skin. Several shot had struck other portions of his hand; one shot had gone into his thigh, another into his ankle. The only serious wound, however, was that which had taken off his finger. I got the lad up, got him to a pool of water, and washed his hand. We clipped away the dangling finger and I tried to assure him that he was not dangerously hurt. His father and the other brother were greatly distressed. The old gentleman said with tears, "Oh, my boy is ruined. He was just getting large enough to help me and now he will never be able to do anything on the farm."

Determined to look on the bright side of the matter, I said to the father, "His finger is gone, but just look what a fine head he has. If he hadn't shot off that finger, he would spend the rest of his life killing tobacco worms and cutting cordwood for the little steamboat that runs up this river. Now, you will have to send him to school, give him an education and some day he will be a great lawyer." I was able to stop their weeping and give them a hopeful view of the situation. The big fine boy looked at me with surprise. His eyes opened wide with interest when I suggested that he get an education and become a lawyer. He wiped away his tears with the shirt sleeve of his uninjured hand and seemed to realize that he was not so badly hurt after all.

They all expressed their gratitude for my coming to them in their trouble. I went to a neighbor's not far away, sent some one in haste for the doctor and went on my way. In course of time, I became an evangelist and went out to hold a meeting in one of the western states. We had quite a large congregation the first night of the services, and while the congregation was singing, just before the benediction I walked down the center aisle, as my custom was, and shook hands with quite a number of people. My attention was especially attracted by a large and very handsome gentleman sitting by an elegantly dressed lady. As I shook hands with him, I said, "Beg pardon, sir, but are you a Christian?" He looked up and smiling said, "No, I am not a Christian, but I am a Kentuckian." He seemed to think that was the next best thing. He said, "I understand you are a Kentuckian and I would be very glad to have you call to see me. I am a lawyer in this town and my office is a certain number on a certain street." I assured him that I would call the next morning.

I was stopping with the pastor of the church where the meetings were being held. After we got home, I told him about meeting this Kentucky lawyer and his invitation to call at his office. The pastor said, "I don't think you want to bother with him. He is one of the most godless men in this town. Did you notice that woman he was with?" "Yes," I said. "Well, that's his wife. Some years ago her first husband died and left a large insurance. The company refused to pay the insurance. She brought suit and employed this Kentucky lawyer. In the course of the trial, the lawyer representing the insurance company made some remark reflecting against the woman who had brought the suit. The Kentucky lawyer gave him a terrible threshing on the spot in spite of the protest of the judge and the officials." "Is that all," I asked. "No," said the preacher, "he won the suit, collected the insurance, and married the woman." I remarked that he was just the kind of fish I was angling for. The pastor thought there was no hope, but I induced him to go around with me the next morning and I found my lawyer seated at the bottom of the stairway leading into his office. He was glad to see me. We went up at once to an elegantly furnished law office. A table sat in the center of the room. He motioned me to a chair on one side while he seated himself in a chair on the other side. The pastor took a newspaper and went over near a window to read the morning news. The lawyer and I got busy talking about Kentucky.

"What county are you from?" I asked.

"Henry County," answered the lawyer.

"In what part of Henry did you live?" I asked.

"Down at the mouth of Sand Riffle Creek on the Kentucky River," was his answer.

"Did you ever know Rev. Peter Kavanaugh?"

"Yes, indeed, he was one of our nearest neighbors and one of the best men in the world."

I remarked that I had known Brother Kavanaugh and while travelling the Jacksonville Circuit had often been entertained in his home. I asked my lawyer how long he had been in Texas, and learned that he had been there some ten years.

I said, "An incident occurred down there close to the mouth of Sand Riffle Creek about fifteen years ago that you may have heard about." I then related to him the story of the boy who shot off his finger and how he had

run and fallen and how I had run through the
fields to get to him, washed his hand and assured him that he was not badly hurt, com-
mented on his fine big head and told him that
he would now go to school and perhaps some
day make a great lawyer. He leaned over the
table and listened with intense interest, looking
me straight in the face. When I got through,
he straightened back in his chair, threw up his
right hand and said, "There's the stump of the
finger!" We leaped to our feet, reached across
the table and caught hold of each other. The
tears came into our eyes. We were bosom
friends from that moment.

He said, "My father and brother have a
large grocery up here on another street and
father has talked many times about the little
man who hitched a gray horse in the lane and
ran to our help. He will be glad to see you."

We went up and met his father. The old
gentleman gave me a cordial greeting; the tears
trickled down his face and we chatted and
laughed together over how my prophecy had
come true. Sure enough, he had sent the boy
to school, he had studied law, gone out to this
western state and had become quite successful

and, as stated before, had won the big insurance case for the widow, whipped the lawyer who had insinuated against her, and married the widow. He would have me down to his home for dinner. He attended the meetings quite regularly and the next summer he and his wife came to the famous old Scottsville Camp.

My lawyer fell under deep conviction for his sins, but would not come to the altar. He said there were some important matters back home he would have to straighten up before he could be a Christian. He went home after the meeting closed and I suppose straightened up matters for he soon professed salvation and united with the Baptist Church.

Some years later, stopping off in the same city I found that he had been elected Mayor and he offered to give a tract of land and build a tabernacle if I would come once a year and hold a camp meeting. I have always been sorry that my time was so crowded with work that I found it impossible to accept his offer. He accumulated considerable property and from time to time when I would meet him in my travels in the West he would always slip his hand into mine with a bill saying that he wanted to help bear my expenses as I carried the good news.

The last time I saw this friend I was passing through St. Louis during the World's Fair in that city and in the great central depot there I met him and his wife. They had just come in from the west to spend some days at the World's Fair. They gave me a most cordial greeting. He moved away from the city where I found him. I do not know where he resides or whether he is living or dead, but, living or dead, we are good friends for time and eternity and I shall never forget the thrill of joy that swept through me when he lifted his hand showing the missing finger and with a smile said, "There's the stump!"

CHAPTER IX

OBEDIENCE TO THE HIGHER LAW

Many years ago, in fact so long ago that I have forgotten the date, I had been engaged by a group of devout people to conduct a holiness convention in one of the Methodist churches in Baltimore. The engagement was standing for several months; I was holding meetings in the East and was to stop off for this convention in Baltimore on my homeward journey; the pastor of the church which had been secured co-operated with the people and we were all looking forward to a gracious time of grace.

The presiding elder of the Baltimore District, however, decided that such conventions would not be for the best interests of the church and community, and notified the pastor that the church must not be used for any such gathering. Of course, the pastor was compelled to obey the dictates of his elder; not to have done so would have been to have been tried at the cabinet meeting of the annual conference, in his absence, behind closed doors, and executed when

75

the appointments were made. Much as it grieved the pastor he was bound to notify the brethren that the convention must be declared off, and they wrote me the circumstances and cancelled the engagement. The elder who prevented our convention, if I remember correctly, was a man named Wilson. He was afterward elected Bishop, and the last I heard of him he was living in the city of New York.

There was a little Mission conducted by holiness people in the city of Baltimore and when they heard I would not be allowed to preach in the church, they wrote asking me to give them the few days that I would have preached in the church. I at once answered their call, and assured them that I would be there. This was not in the spirit of lawlessness, but it was obedience to the higher law. I had, as I still have, a profound conviction that God would have me preach full redemption from sin here and now, through faith in our Lord and Saviour Jesus Christ; and always when I have been convinced that church officials sought to use their authority to prevent my preaching this full salvation to the people, I have felt compelled to listen to the voice of the Spirit and obey the higher law.

I remember to have heard a prominent preacher of the church of which I am a member say that, "The voice of the church is the voice of God to me." That sounds to me very much like Roman Catholicism. I think I have heard certain church officials do a good deal of talking for which neither the church nor God would be willing to be held responsible. It is quite possible for men to get into places of authority in the church who know nothing of the true bride of Christ, who have had much to say with reference to ecclesiastical affairs, who never uttered a sentence for the bride of Christ, or under the leadership of the Holy Ghost, in their lives. There is certainly much talk going on by various church officials today that thoughtful and devout men would not dare to believe God has anything to do with.

I went and held the convention in a little Mission around the corner. The people were frightened, the attendance was not large; some of them seemed to think I had committed a great sin in daring to come into a city over the protest of the presiding elder. But a number of humble people gathered at these meetings; there was earnest prayer, hungry hearts were fed, and we were all blessed together. Through a long and varied experience I have found that when we meet together with sincere hearts, under the strong opposition of the opposers of the doctrine of full salvation, we are blessed in a most signal and gracious manner. Somehow, when we are cut off from human sympathy and help it drives us to God in deep humility, earnest prayer, and humble trust in a very peculiar way, and the results are most gratifying.

Sinners were converted, backsliders were reclaimed and believers were sanctified. The remuneration in dollars and cents was very small, but the blessing of the Lord upon my own soul was very gracious; and there was some abiding fruit.

I remember very well that one evening after the meetings had closed, a very handsome boy, with an unusually classic and pure face, came to me and looking up with an eagerness that profoundly impressed me said, "I feel that I am called to preach the gospel. I desire to go to school where I can be educated and be prepared to preach in a spiritual atmosphere; a safe place for the development of my soul and spiritual life, along with my intellectual training."

I said to him without hesitation, "Asbury College at Wilmore, Ky., is the very place you are seeking." I directed him with reference to correspondence and how to find Wilmore. In due time the young brother showed up on the campus at Asbury, was enrolled, and turned out to be a very excellent student. At first, he was not favorably impressed with some of the joyful manifestations of other students, but in due time fell under deep conviction for full salvation and received a gracious baptism with the Holy Ghost in sanctifying power.

He at once took front rank in the spiritual life of the school and was a real factor in the intellectual and religious activities of the student body. He soon felt a call to the mission field and took a very active part in the organization and work of the missionary society. He was a good speaker and was often heard on the college platform, and frequently went out into the community to preach and speak on the subject of missions. There has rarely been a student in Asbury College who wielded a larger and more wholesome influence than this same young man whom I had met in the little mission around the corner in the holiness convention in Baltimore.

Immediately after graduation he went out to the vast mission field of India, and when I was making my tour of the world I found him laboring successfully among the Hindu people. He had acquired the language in a remarkable degree. He was a sort of John Fletcher among the missionaries, and though quite young, his spiritual influence was being felt, not only among the Methodist people but among the devout missionaries of all churches. He was a modest man, with saintly appearance, beautiful voice, and a courtesy and kindness that won the respect and confidence of all with whom he came in contact. It was frequently whispered to me that he was wielding a wider and more profound spiritual influence than any other man in India.

During the several furloughs of this brother in the homeland he has been able to wield a very wide and powerful influence on the home church; and in fact, has become one of the best known and most loved men in Methodism. He has been enabled to arouse thousands of people, not only to more liberal giving, but to a better understanding of the whole spirit of missions, and a deeper consciousness of their obligations to spread the gospel of our Lord Jesus throughout the world. Being a member of the General Conference at one time, his brethren would have thrust upon him the office of Bishop, which, after earnest prayer, he positively refused, saying, he much preferred to remain an evangelist among the great people of India where God had given him open doors and the open hearts of a countless multitude of people.

I claim no credit whatever, for the splendid character and remarkable ministry of this man, but I have asked myself what the results might have been had I not disregarded the orders of the presiding elder and obeyed the higher orders —the voice of God in my soul. If I had not gone to this little Mission and directed this young man's steps to Asbury College where he was graciously sanctified and called into the mission field, would he have been the tremendous power in India, and the man of wide influence in the church today that he is? Had he gone to some school where he would have been taught that Moses did not write the Pentateuch, that Daniel was a myth, that it was of no real consequence whether our Lord Jesus was of virgin birth or the son of Joseph, that regeneration was not necessary, that moral and mental training would enable one to meet all the emergencies of life and all the requirements of God, that sanctification was a mere religious hysteria, that the Bible perhaps contained the word of God, but was no longer to be regarded as a divine revelation—I say, had he gone to such a school, could he possibly have become the man he is, and have performed the great work that, under God, has been brought about through his ministry—Impossible!

In view of these facts, I am profoundly grateful that I disregarded the orders of man and listened to the voice of God. In the course of my ministry it has frequently become my duty to follow this course, never in the spirit of lawlessness or daring, but always under a profound conviction that God was leading, and that I must go forward or grieve the Holy Spirit.

Once, while holding meetings in a village in Texas, I received a letter cancelling an engagement in another state, but I was so profoundly impressed that I should go forward that, for many mornings after breakfast I went away to a quiet place in a pine forest and laid the matter before God in prayer. One morning the Lord met me there very graciously and as I walked up and down amid the trees rejoicing, the Spirit spoke very distinctly within me these words, "I have set before thee an open door, and no man can shut it." This gave me great comfort and courage. I went into the state where my engagement had been cancelled, found many open doors and was blessed in preaching full redemption in Jesus. I have never sought to force doors open, but have never feared to enter doors that God had opened, whatever opposition men might offer.

P. S.—The man to whom I refer in this chapter is Rev. E. Stanley Jones, D.D.

CHAPTER X

ENTERING THE MINISTRY ON HORSEBACK

It may be interesting to the reader to learn something of the immediate cause of my entering the ministry. I felt the call to preach when quite young, and soon after my conversion became a zealous and successful worker in revival meetings.

I set up the family altar in my grandfather's home where I was raised, when about fifteen years of age, and it was understood in all the country round that "Bud" Morrison would preach. "Bud" was my nickname, and many of the people of the neighborhood did not know I had any other name until I was grown and went back to preach to them.

My whole heart was aglow with the thought of preaching the gospel when, in the fall of 1874, I left Barren County, Ky., for Boyle County to live with my mother's people. The change in my environment was very marked. I found much more of the world and less of

spiritual ardor in the Blue Grass than I had left
in the broom sedge. No one seemed to take an
interest in my soul. I had my church letter, but
no one suggested that I put it in the church.
For a year I remained out of the church, and
of course did not grow in grace; meanwhile,
the world was after me hotfoot. I must go to
every party, be at every picnic, and you may
be sure the young sinners in the community did
not neglect me, and were very interesting.

I attended school at Ewing Institute in Perryville, Ky., joined the debating society, practiced
speaking before the public, excited some interest, and was developing somewhat along that
line. When I quit school in the spring I remained a member of the debating club, prepared my speeches between the plow handles
and walked into Perryville to debate one night
in the week, and won every time. The silence
of the field, the murmuring song of the plow
helped me to think, often becoming so stirred
with my subject that I would speak aloud as I
strode after "Old Ransom," a faithful horse,
between the corn rows. The hardest and most
exacting man I ever worked for said I could

plow more corn in a day than any boy he had ever hired. I received for my wages, ten dollars per month and table board. But you must not forget that my cornfield was my "school of expression," and I may add to this that, I sang or whistled most of the time when not preparing and practicing speeches for the debate, and in this way I was unconsciously developing a strong pair of lungs for camp meetings to come. My success in the debates was such that people began to say, "If we do not license Henry Morrison to preach he will go to Congress." This sounded good in the ears of a plowboy.

My relatives about Perryville were a bit amused at my thought of preaching. They said the "G. P.," I had seen in my night vision meant "go plow." My full name was Henry Clay Poverty. Ten dollars a month was slow going. Think of ten months of hard work, up at dawn, and hard at it until after dark. Speaking of white slavery, I know what it is. When the corn was laid by I worked at what I could find, trimmed hedges, scattered sand on the pike, cut cordwood, etc. The old hand that guides this pen has cut many a cord of wood; good ex-

ercise strengthening the fiber for the strenuous
work of evangelism.

In spite of the many handicaps, much dis-
couragement and not a little ridicule, my mind
was fully made up to preach, but there seemed
no special need for hurry. I had a cousin, a fine
young fellow, Jimmie Reins, who also was an
orphan boy, and we chummed and played together.

Meanwhile, Rev. T. F. Taliaferro was sent to
the Perryville Circuit, and he at once became
my friend. I was often at the parsonage, and
Bro. Taliaferro inspired me with new hope. He
held a revival in which I was greatly blessed,
and while I took a deep interest in the church
work, seeing the very poor support of the ministry, I thought it would be a good idea to make
and lay by a snug sum of money before devot-
ing my life to preaching. My cousin Jimmie
and I concluded that the quickest and most interesting way to make a fortune would be to
go to Texas and go into the cattle business. We
had no money to invest in cattle, but that was
a small matter; we would be cowboys for
awhile, save our wages, buy some cattle, and

soon be successful cattle men. Youth, ambition, faith in ourselves, we felt success was awaiting us and urging us to hasten to Texas.

In the midst of our planning a man came to Perryville, rented an empty store, covered one side of the wall with pictures; printed in loud colors, were mountains in Switzerland, castles on the Rhine in Germany, landscapes in England, valleys in Italy—a world of pictures! He arranged a light with a reflector on the opposite side of the store which threw a glare of light on the pictures. He had his sales at night when everything showed up to best advantage. The people crowded the place and the salesman with most cultured voice and graceful use of a long wand, pointed out the attractive features of his works of art. The people bought them in large numbers. Cousin Jimmie and I saw a fortune much nearer home than Texas, and much quicker than raising longhorned steers. We agreed to go into the picture business, and sent away and got a number of cheap samples from which to select our stock.

Meanwhile, I was breaking a big young horse to the saddle for a neighbor boy. He was an immense animal, hard-mouthed, and contrary. I rode this young horse into Perryville to get my sample pictures and was returning to the country with the pictures in a large haversack strapped over my shoulder. As I rode out of the village I was holding the bridle rein in my left hand and holding an apple in my right hand, from which I was taking an occasional bite. The horse commenced to rear and prance about and try to run. I had to drop the apple in order to use both hands on the bridle; when the half-eaten apple struck the ground it frightened the horse and he leaped forward with such violence that my hat fell off and struck him behind the saddle. This added to his fright and he stretched himself for the run of his life. In plunging forward he had jerked my left foot from the stirrup and thrown me entirely out of the saddle, perching me up on the saddle horn. I had no control of the situation; the bridle reins were loose and it was with great difficulty that I kept from falling from my elevated and uncomfortable perch. We were traveling up a gradual incline for some two hundred yards, then we would pass over the brow of the hill and go down a steep grade. I felt sure when we started down that grade I would be dashed to death. As we turned over the hill I looked down at the hard stone pike and it seemed a long way off, and my death seemed certain.

Right there, in my heart, I entered the ministry, provided that horse ever stopped running, and I was not killed. I lost interest in Texas cattle, and entirely gave up the picture business. I had no desire to be rich. I wanted to be a preacher of the gospel. I lost sight of the financial feature; to be a poor, earnest preacher was good enough for me. My decision was full and final. In less than a minute I was firmly seated in the saddle, my horse was under control, and in the mad dash of those few hundred yards I had been changed from an enterprising cattleman or an extensive dealer in fine art into an humble, contented circuit rider. But for the runaway horse I might have drifted from one adventure to another, and finally fallen entirely away from Christ, never have entered the ministry and, in the end, lost my soul. Thank God for the wild ride that landed me in the ministry.

Soon after this experience I was licensed to

preach, and found myself the assistant preacher on a large circuit; having no horse, I walked the rounds and I doubt if I have ever been happier in my life than when striding along the dusty roads and short cuts across the fields to my Sunday appointments. Many times during my long ministry I have looked back to that wild ride and felt profoundly grateful to God for the frightened horse, and have been able to sympathize somewhat with Jonah; in his case it was a fish; in my case it was a runaway horse.

CHAPTER XI
PLOWING DEEP

I have somewhere read a story told by Mr. Stanley to the effect that, while searching for Dr. Livingstone in Africa, he halted his caravan and went into camp to await the coming of certain provisions. While in camp he determined to clear up a piece of ground and plant some corn.

Stanley says that during his travels in Africa he was surprised that he did not see more snakes; he was expecting to find the forests and jungles of Africa alive with them; but as he passed along he saw but few snakes. However, when he commenced clearing the ground to raise corn he found snakes everywhere; snakes up the trees, snakes in the hollow logs, snakes under the rocks, snakes in the grass; when they put the plow into the ground they turned up snakes; they had an immense snake killing but they soon had corn tall enough to hide an elephant. If they had not cleared the land to raise the corn they would have had no idea of the abundance of snakes.

This interesting incident of Stanley's in Africa suggested to me that the minister of the gospel may have little, or no accurate knowledge of the sinful conditions of a community until, with the ax of the law, he falls to hewing down the jungles of sin and puts the gospel plow deep into the moral soil of the community. The word of God faithfully preached will bring to light the secrets hidden deep in the human soul. Under such circumstances there will very likely be the hissing and anger of the carnal serpents of sin; there will also be the cry of the wounded begging for help and deliverance from sin. It is of the greatest importance that the preacher of the gospel clear the moral jungles about him; that he faithfully proclaim to the people the sinfulness of sin, the danger of it, God's hatred of it, and the fearful judgment it will bring upon the impenitent. The preacher should call sins by their names; he ought to cry out very plainly against lying, stealing, deception, tattling, dishonesty, Sabbath breaking, uncleanness of every kind, and in this way bring home to the heart and conscience of all classes of sinners their individual wickedness and thus arouse their conscience to their danger, ferret out and condemn the thing of which they are guilty, and from which they must be saved or lost forever.

This is not abusing sinners; it is far from it; it is being faithful to them. It should be done in the spirit of love for the sinner, but of severity against his sins. Men cannot be saved without repentance, and they are not likely to repent without their sins in their heinousness being put in their true light under the glare of the gospel.

Nothing can be more unfortunate for the preacher and the people to whom he ministers than that he should comfort them in their sins instead of so condemning their sins that he will arouse in them conviction, bring them to repentance and lead them out of their sins. There is one thing of which the preacher may be sure in any community; there are sinners all about him. There is deep, hidden, well-dressed selfishness; dishonesty in trade, disobedience to parents, profanity, hatred, backbiting, envy, impurity of thought and desire. You can hardly find a community in which there are not vulgar vices which need to be exposed and rebuked with great earnestness.

This being true, if the minister will be faithful to God who has sent him, and the people to whom he preaches, he must smite sin with fearless earnestness; he must let no class of sinners escape. While his heart is full of tenderness and pity for the sinner, he must be so severe against the sin that the sinner will realize its heinousness, fall out with it, forsake it, and cry to God for the forgiveness of it.

I can but believe that there is a very weak place just at this point in much of our present-day preaching. Of course, the minister loves the people to whom he preaches, but that love must urge him on to try, by all means, to bring about their repentance and salvation. There is no more admirable man than the honest, courageous, faithful man in the pulpit who will "Cry aloud, and spare not." He is full of compassion, he has the tenderest solicitude, and the power of God is upon him. His heart is on fire with love for souls. They must be awakened; they must be brought to repentance. His responsibility is great; he must give an account before God in the day of judgment. He is not simply an entertainer; he is not to build up and preserve his reputation as a great orator or profound scholar. He may be a scholar, he may be eloquent, but his scholarship and eloquence must be consecrated to one great end — the awakening of sinners, bringing them to repentance, and winning them to saving faith in Christ.

Any minister lacking in courage at this point, or fearful that the people will not endure sound doctrine and close, searching preaching, is mistaken. People, generally, have a very good idea of what the preacher ought to be, and what he ought to say; and the people admire a fearless, earnest, loving, gospel preacher. If he speaks with holy courage in an intelligent, positive way, it is quite probable that some whose hearts are set to do evil, will resist him, refuse to hear or support him; but the majority of the people of any community will hear his message, many will heed his warning, and be saved through his faithful ministry.

Remember, if Mr. Stanley had not cleared the ground he would not have found the snakes. Do not forget that he would not have raised the corn. If we desire a harvest of souls for Christ we must have the courage to clear up the moral jungles and kill the snakes of sin. In the times in which we are living there is quite a bit of sowing of religious seed in uncleared and unbroken land. The preacher who fails to attack sin, who does not insist on supreme surrender to Christ, on the forsaking of the world, taking up the cross and following the divine Master, may receive the plaudits and approval of a people who love the world, who enjoy its pleasures, and who know nothing of a life of crucifixion, of holy communion and fellowship with the blessed Trinity, but what about the harvest! What about this minister and his people in the great day of accounts!

There has never been a time in the religious history of this country when there was greater need for true heroes in our pulpits; men who have paid the supreme price, whose lives are hid with Christ in God, who are not seeking ecclesiastical office, the money or the applause of the people to whom they may preach, but who are mad against sin, who have gone to war against Satan, his devices and delusions, whose one great object is the rescue of souls and the presenting of them perfect in holiness at the coming of our blessed Lord and Master.

CHAPTER XII

THE OLD COLORED PREACHER

I have always loved colored people. They have been wonderfully good to me. When my mother died, I was two years of age. My father took me to live with my Grandfather Morrison. He took along with me, as my caretaker, a stout colored boy named Frank. I know nothing of the history of this boy up to that time. He lived with me at my Grandfather's for quite a while. He carried me on his shoulders when I was tired. He carried me in his arms when I was sleepy. He sat on the floor at my side while I ate my meals. If milk was scarce, I left one-half of the milk in my glass for Frank. A child never had a better friend. That boy loved, cared for and guarded me. If he has passed on, I do hope to meet him in Heaven. If he is still living I wish I knew where he is and it would be a great delight to smooth his pathway a bit in his old age.

When the wife of my youth died, she left me three children, all of them very young. Joe, the faithful colored man, came to the back door of our house and asked the privilege to come into the death chamber and look on the dead face of "Miss Laura." He wept with me and comforted me. He was in the employment of Colonel Geo. W. Bain, the great champion of Prohibition and the charming Chautauqua lecturer. My children went to live with my father-in-law, Colonel Bain. Joe was Mr. Bain's carriage driver and man about the place. He loved my children. When he rode the horses about for their exercise or went for the cows, the older little boy rode behind him, the younger one on a pillow in his lap. When I would leave for meetings, he would drive me out to the station and I would say, "Joe, take good care of the children." And he would answer with unctuous emphasis, "I sho will!" He was faithful and loyal, *and me not love Joe!* I haven't seen or heard of him for many years. I think he is dead. I trust he is in Heaven. If he is, I shall be glad to have a long, good talk with him when I get home.

Once when I was a poor orphan boy, I lived with an old bachelor. He had many colored people on the place and he and I were the only white persons. Our bill of fare was very plain. He was a close-fisted old man and a bit exacting. He spent much of his time away from home trading and left me alone with the colored people. It was one of the most dangerous periods of my life. In those days, I carried a Smith and Wesson, Number Thirty-two, in my hip pocket and became quite expert shooting at the blossom end of pumpkins in the corn-fields and at spots on beech trees and white sycamore limbs. The old colored people on the place were solicitous about me and spoke words of sympathy and caution. Many a time after the frugal meal in the big house, I went down in the back yard to Aunt Mandy's cabin. She always had something nice for me; sometimes, it was the tender leg of a fried chicken; sometimes it was a big piece of delicious ginger bread; sometimes, it was pumpkin pie with the pumpkin so deep that when I bit off a piece my nose marked off the next bite.

I could tell of other colored people who have helped me along the way of life, whose kindnesses and courtesies have been a real blessing to me. I have preached for them often and had some gracious times. Frequently, during our battle for Prohibition in Kentucky, I was sent for to come to various county seats and speak to the colored people. They always gathered in large numbers to hear me and I was always able to arouse their enthusiasm against the saloon, their worst enemy. It was delightful to go into a town and speak two or three nights to the colored people, stir up their religious emotion and see them march up to the polls and hit old whiskey a good death blow.

But, to get back to my old colored preacher. It was while I was pastor in Frankfort, Ky. I frequently preached for the colored folks. One evening, I was passing by the colored Baptist Church; they were having a revival. I stepped in and sat on the back seat. In those days, colored preachers were very fond of preaching on "The deliverance of Israel from bondage." They had not been so long out of slavery and seemed to see a sort of parallel between themselves, their deliverance from bondage, and that of the ancient Hebrew people. The old colored preacher, as I stepped into the church, was crying out, in a loud, mellow, voice, "Moses went up on de mountain, and he stayed dar, and he stayed dar; and dem Hebrew chillun din' know whar

he wuz gone. But he stayed dar, and he stayed
dar, and dey sho' didn't know what had become o' Moses, who had promised to lead dem
to de promised lan'. But Moses, he stayed up
in de mountain a-communin' wid de Lawd.
And when he did come down, he come wid de
shine on him, and when dem chillun saw de
shine on him, dey knowed whar he'd been, and
dey sho follered dat man because it wuz plain
to dem he had been on de mountain wid de
Lawd. Look heah, people, ef you wants de sinner to foller you into de Kingdom, you got ter
go up into de mountain and stay wid de Lawd.
Better git on yo' knees and stay dar, and stay
dar, tell you gits de shine on you. Den it'll be
time enough for you to come down, and den
de po' sinners will know whar you been, and
dey will sho' foller you into de Kingdom."

I have never forgotten that old colored
preacher's exhortation. He was quite correct.
Let the people know that a man has been up
on the mountain with God. Let them know
that his heart is pure, that his motives are un-
selfish, that his one great consuming desire is
their salvation and happiness here and hereafter,
and they will follow him.

CHAPTER VIII

"A CITY SET ON AN HILL"

The first station I ever served as a minister of the Gospel was Stanford, Ky. It is the county seat of Lincoln County, in the edge of the Blue Grass. Stanford is a beautiful little city; a more delightful people cannot be found anywhere. It was my first love among all the county seats, towns and cities in which I've preached in almost fifty years of my ministry.

When I got to Stanford, I found a boarding house with a most delightful family. Rev. John Bruce, a lovely Christian gentleman and single man, was pastor of the Baptist Church and was boarding with the same family. When I enquired after the spiritual state of the community, Brother Bruce said, "The spiritual life here is none too good. We need a revival." He said, "There is a wonderful woman down here at the toll gate on the Crab Orchard Pike. Her name is Mary McAfee. She is a very remarkable Christian; a little peculiar in her views, but

103

wonderfully filled with the Spirit. If we had more like her, the churches would be in much better condition. She is a member of your church."

Rev. Mr. McElroy was the pastor of the Presbyterian Church. He called to see me a few days after my arrival. He was a most delightful Christian gentleman. He talked very earnestly about the great need of a revival in the town. By and by, he said, "Have you met Mary McAfee? She is a member of your congregation. She keeps the toll gate down here on the Crab Orchard Pike, something more than half a mile out. You must call to see her. She is a remarkable saint, has some queer notions, but has a wonderful experience. She claims an experience of full salvation and she certainly lives very close to her Lord."

A few days after landing in Stanford, I found, from reading the town paper, that there were twenty-eight prisoners in the county jail. I got permission from the jailer to preach to them. Most all of them were colored men. They seemed to appreciate my visit and sermon very much. Several of them Amen-ed me very heartily. After preaching, I chatted with them awhile. Among other things, I asked, "What is the spiritual state of this community?" They all laughed and their spokesman, whom I afterward found was a steward in the colored Methodist Church in the town, said, "Boss, dis ain't no place fer you to come, lookin' aftah de spiritual state o' de town. If we had knowed mo' about dat and less about some other things, we wouldn't be whar we is. Dey ain't much religion in dis heah place. I will say dey *is* a saint down at de toll gate. Dis heah Mis' McAfee, she sho' lives wid de Lawd. Dat woman is got Bible ligion."

You may be sure I was becoming deeply interested in Sister McAfee. I went down to see her. I found a very modest, little maiden woman. She must have been past forty years of age. She told me a wonderful story of how she had received the baptism with the Holy Spirit in sanctifying power, how that after being bedridden for seven years, she had been instantly healed, and how the Lord had been graciously using her in the salvation of souls. I had never met in all my life with any one to whom Jesus Christ seemed a more real person and a more gracious and present Saviour. The tears trickled down my cheeks while she talked. I asked for an interest in her prayers and went away profoundly impressed.

There was a skeptic in the town (you will always find one in a County Seat or village). I went up to his office and had a talk with him. He was a bit sour; he criticised the religious life of some of the men in the churches. He was disposed to find fault. I was a bit embarrassed. By and by he said, "There is a little woman by the name of McAfee that keeps the toll gate down on the Crab Orchard Pike. If I could get the kind of religion she has, I would like to have it." I remembered that my Master had likened a consecrated, holy life to a "city set on a hill that could not be hid."

When ministers would visit me, I would take them down to the toll gate and ask Sister McAfee to tell her experience. Every one who heard her was profoundly impressed. She was never excited and never afraid. She was resting in the calm of full redemption and perfect love. Her education was very limited, but her comprehen-

sion of scriptural truth was very remarkable
and her thinking wonderfully clear. She prayed
very earnestly that I might be wholly consecrated, entirely saved from sin, and filled with
the Holy Ghost. She was a power in our revivals. Everybody believed in her. Her testimonies were quiet and convincing. She walked
with God. She breathed the spirit of prayer,
forgiveness and love. The people who came in
contact with her longed to know more about
Jesus.

A newspaper reporter went down and had a
talk with her, gave her testimony to the *Courier-
Journal*. Rev. W. W. Hopper, down in Mississippi, read her testimony and came to Stanford
to ask her about her experience and ask for her
prayers. While there, he received the baptism
with the Holy Spirit in sanctifying power. He
returned to Mississippi to preach a full salvation in Christ received now by faith. Dr. Car-
radine was brought into this gracious experience under the ministry of Brother Hopper.
The fire spread. It would take a bookcase full
of books to tell the wondrous story of how the
fire spread, sinners were converted, preachers

were sanctified, missionaries went out over the seas. The years passed; little Mary's health failed and she faded gradually and then her saintly spirit, on wings of love and faith, rose to meet and dwell with her blessed Saviour forevermore.

The good people of Stanford sent for me to say some words at her funeral service. As I stood by the plain coffin and looked at her quiet, saintly face that seemed to tell of a soul that had entered into eternal rest, I hadn't a doubt but directly and indirectly a hundred thousand souls had been touched for good through the holy life and the beautiful testimony of a little maiden woman who kept the toll gate on the Crab Orchard Turnpike in the outskirts of Stanford, Ky. There are no mathematics with which we can estimate the value of a wholly consecrated, beautifully sanctified, consistent life with a glad testimony to the saving and keeping power of our blessed Lord and Saviour, Jesus Christ.

CHAPTER XIV

MY ARREST AND RESCUE

It was during Christmas week that I was placed under arrest and dragged into court. I was a very small boy, in my fourteenth year; I would be fourteen years of age the tenth of the coming March. I was caught in the act; there was no excuse, there seemed to be no help or hope. I was guilty, I was thrust into the prisoners' dock, the gate was slammed, and a big policeman leaned on the gate, and seemed to look at me with a degree of satisfaction at the thought that he had me, and that I was sure of punishment.

I felt utterly helpless; I could not even weep, I had wept all the tears out of my system; I was dry and emotionless, except I was crushed to the very earth with a sense of my guilt and lostness. The judge was in his big chair but I did not dare look at him. I had no hope for mercy, and I knew that justice would be my ruin.

The courthouse was packed with people; they were gazing at me, as I crouched in the corner of the dock, with looks of accusation which seemed to say, Judge, give him the full benefit of the law and save society from further trouble. Finally, the clerk announced the opening of the court and my case came first. The judge asked the clerk if the boy had any one to represent him. Represent was a new word to me; I supposed my representative was to be my executioner. The clerk answered that I had no one. The judge then said to a lawyer within the bar, I appoint you to represent this boy. The lawyer arose and walking slowly forward, picking his way among the chairs, approached the dock, pushed the policeman to one side, opened the gate and stepped inside the dock. I, withered with fear, crouched closely in my corner, and with eyes wide open with horror, gazed up at my lawyer. He had a wonderful face; it was strong and calm, full of kindness and marvelous beauty. I noticed a tear hanging on his eyelashes; that tear helped me wonderfully. He sat down and slipped his arm around me. It seemed that my very bones had dropped out of their sockets and I was scarcely breathing below my collar button. My attorney drew me up to him; the pressure was so gentle, and yet so strong, it seemed to restore and readjust my bones, relax my nerves, and I commenced to breathe more deeply. Stooping down his silken beard brushed over my suntanned face, and placing his lips close to my ear, he said, "My little friend, are you guilty?" I could not have lied to him if it had been to save my life. With trembling voice I answered, "Yes sir, I am guilty of much more than they know about." "Well," said he, "do you not think it will be best for us to confess judgment and throw you on the mercy of the court?" I did not know what it meant to be thrown on the mercy of the court, but I felt sure that if he would throw me I would alight in the best place there was for me, and I at once answered in the affirmative. My lawyer gave me a gentle pat on the head, and stood up facing the judge.

He said: "Please your Honor, it has been my privilege to practice for many years in your Honor's court, and I have been glad to notice that when the ends of justice can be secured, and society can be protected, it has been your Honor's prerogative to show mercy. I thank the court for appointing me to plead in the interest of this little boy. He confesses his guilt. His heart is broken, he is full of contrition; he has been an orphan from his infancy and is dependent and moneyless, and begs for compassion."

I reached out my soiled, lean fingers and caught hold of the skirt of my attorney's coat. I clung to him with the feeling that if I would hold onto him he would pull me out. I thought his speech was finished but it was a mere introduction. A deep stillness fell upon the great gathering of people and his mellow voice rose until it filled the great room with a most marvelous appeal. He spoke of orphan children, of their loneliness, of their unprotected condition, of the temptations to which they were subjected, of their desolation, like lambs without a shepherd in a world full of hungry wolves seeking to destroy. He spoke until the harsh people softened, old men groaned aloud. He spoke until the tears trickled down the policeman's cheek and looking kindly at me he whispered to know if I did not want a drink of water. I was too busy clinging to the coat-tail of my attorney, gazing into his wonderful face, and listening to his marvelous words, to want anything else. I was breathing deep, new life and hope were creeping into me. I was falling desperately in love with my lawyer.

My attorney said, "Please your Honor, if you in the spirit of mercy, will dismiss the charges and set the lad free, I pledge myself to become his guardian, to see to it that he has a home and protection. I will look after his education and I promise to give to society a good and useful citizen."

I could scarcely keep from crying aloud for joy. It seemed my heart would burst within me for gratitude. I felt as if they would let me place my ragged shoes upon the bench upon which I sat, and throw my ragged coat sleeve about the neck of my attorney and kiss his cheek one time, they might take me out and hang me, and I would die shouting.

In the midst of his wonderful address my attorney, instead of addressing the judge as "Your Honor," said, "My Father." This shot through me. I saw that if the judge had appointed his own son to plead for me it was more than likely that he would heed his pleadings and show me mercy. Men were weeping all over the courthouse. I had both hands full of the skirts of the coat of my lawyer; the policeman had laid aside his cap, had gotten out his handkerchief, and had buried his face in a flood of tears. It was a powerful moment in my trial; my attorney had reached his climax. He exclaimed, "My father, this child for whom I plead is none other than my brother." I saw at once that if the judge was the father of my attorney, and the attorney was my brother, then the judge was my father also. I could restrain myself no longer. I gave a great cry of joy, leaped out of the dock, rushed up into the judge's stand and flung myself upon his bosom. He embraced me with a long, tender pressure that seemed to make me through and through a new creature. Folding me in his arms he stood up and said, "Rejoice with me, for my son who was dead is alive, who was lost is found." The entire crowd in the courthouse broke into tears and laughter. The people embraced each other; they all seemed to want to shake hands with me. They congratulated my attorney, and we laughed, and wept, and shouted together.

I hardly need tell you that the courthouse was a Methodist Church, that the trial was an old-time revival, that the Word of God arrested me and brought me, convicted and guilty, to the bar of justice; that the eternal Father was the Judge upon the throne, and that the Lord Jesus Christ was the attorney who pled my case, won my pardon, and secured my eternal salvation.

I look back with fondest memory to that great occasion when bowed and burdened with guilt, bound with sin, Jesus Christ undertook for me, broke my chains, swept away my guilt, and at the throne of the universe secured for me a full and free forgiveness, a blessed and glorious pardon, and revealed the blessed fact that the great God—the Judge of all the world —was, and is, my Father in heaven.

CHAPTER XV

SAVED TO SERVE

"I pray not that thou shouldest take them out of the world, but that thou shouldest keep them from the evil one"—John 17:15.

The seventeenth chapter of John contains the Lord's Prayer. It is very common to call that beautiful form of prayer which the Lord gave us for our use, beginning with "Our Father who art in heaven," and saying "after this manner, therefore, pray ye," the Lord's Prayer. That is a mistake; it is our prayer given us by our Lord; not that we should continually use these words and no others, but it is the general form of prayer that we should use, recognizing God as our Father, praying His kingdom to come on earth, asking the forgiveness of our sins, pledging ourselves to forgive those who sin against us, also looking to Him to supply our daily needs, etc.

Our Lord's Prayer, the prayer He offered for Himself, His disciples, and all who should believe on Him through their word, is contained in the seventeenth chapter of John's gospel. It should be observed that in the beginning of this prayer our Lord speaks of the relationship which exists between Him and His Father, and asks the Father to glorify Him. He speaks of the power that the Father has given Him over all flesh, to give eternal life to men. He also mentions the fact that this eternal life is to be obtained through Himself. He then speaks of the relationship existing between Himself and His disciples.

He begins His prayer for His disciples in the ninth verse, and it is quite interesting to notice that this prayer is offered exclusively for the disciples. "I pray for them: I pray not for the world, but for them which thou hast given me; for they are thine." Jesus was having a special prayer meeting with the disciples and was laying the foundation for His church under the new dispensation. He came to taste death for every man, to offer salvation to whosoever will, but just now He is not praying for the world at large, that is, the unregenerated, the impenitent, those who have not come out of the world, the sinful and lost multitudes, but He is praying for this little group that the Father had given Him who are His in the most special and sacred sense.

Our Lord wants a church separated from all wicked worldliness, redeemed, cleansed, filled, set apart, and wholly His, worthy witnesses of His divine Sonship, saving grace, and good samples of His power to save. Jesus wants a holy church; a great spiritual, dynamic force in the world; a church which is His bride in deed and in truth. He came to taste death for every man. His mission was to the entire world; He commanded His disciples to carry His message to every creature, to bear their witness to the "uttermost parts of the earth." This upper room prayer meeting was held with His disciples; with a saved people, with the seed corn, if you will, of a new dispensation. He wanted them to be saved to the uttermost, to be emptied of all sin, and to be kept from any taint of unrighteousness, and mighty witness of His redeeming power.

God works through human instrumentality, and He cannot save sinners out in the world through the influence of sinners in the church.

The worst of sinners are church sinners claiming to be Christians when they are not. Give God a church separate from the world and filled with the Holy Ghost, true witnesses of the power of Christ, and He can move mightily upon the world to bring the lost to salvation; but fill up the church with unregenerated, sinful people and that sort of church is utterly helpless to save the lost, neither can God work through that sort of church to save sinners. Let the church be the true, regenerated, sanctified, spiritual bride of the Lord Jesus and children will be born into the kingdom and nurtured upon the bosom of the church, fed with the sincere milk of the word, and they will grow into men and women in Christ.

We shall not undertake a comment on this entire prayer, but wish to call special attention to the fifteenth verse. Read it: "I pray not that thou shouldest take them out of the world, but that thou shouldest keep them from the evil." The revised version has it, "Keep them from the *evil one*." Deliver and keep them from the temptations of the devil, the defilement of sin. Give them protection against any and all powers that would soil their souls, or hinder them from being true witnesses and good examples of my power to save the people from their sins.

It will be understood that when our Lord says, "I pray not that thou shouldest take them out of the world," He is not speaking of the sinful or unregenerate world, but He is saying that He does not desire them now to be translated into heaven, but left for service among men.

God's program in the salvation of souls is to take men out of the world, out from among the rebellious and sinful, then to take the world out of them, to cleanse out of them the pride of life, the spirit of covetousness, of hatred, to purify their hearts, to fill them with the Holy Spirit, and then to send them back into the unregenerated world to witness to it, to rebuke it, to warn it, to call it to repentance, and to promise it full salvation through faith in Christ.

Let me illustrate: Some years ago there came a handsome, wicked young man out of Cincinnati over into the beautiful hills of Kentucky. There he found, wooed, and won the heart of a beautiful country girl. She loved him devotedly, and trusted him implicitly. He enticed her into Cincinnati with the promise of marriage. He took her over the Rhine, blighted her life, broke her heart, laughed at her for her credulity, and flung her away to the beasts of sin. She was ashamed to go back to her parents and went down into the lowest depths. For some years she lived in the haunts of vice; she became a drunkard; she cursed and swore and fought in the back alleys of the slums. She was found wasting with sickness and polluted with sin. Some good women took her to a place of refuge, led her to repentance and saving faith in Christ, nursed her back to health, and again the roses bloomed in her cheeks and joy and praise came into her heart. Her parents were written to and in due time she was shipped back across the river to her old Kentucky home.

Her father, a devout old farmer, met her at the station with his spring wagon, took her tenderly to his heart, loaded her trunk, seated her by his side, and they trotted away down the beautiful lanes, with the apple trees blooming and the birds singing on every side. It seemed as if she had fallen asleep and awakened in paradise. Her mother received her with unutterable gladness. Her room upstairs was prepared in the most perfect order, flowers on the dresser welcomed her. The days passed with inexpressible happiness. The darling daughter, the only child of the family, lamented as dead and lost, had come back home bright and beautiful, saved and rejoicing.

Some weeks passed away and the mother missing the daughter for some time, went up to her room and found her on her knees at the bedside in an agony of prayer and tears. She said, "Daughter, have you lost your peace with God, your communion with Jesus?" "Oh, no, mother, I have never had a sweeter experience than at the present time, but I shall have to leave you. I am going back to Cincinnati."

"My darling," cried her mother, catching her in her arms, "you have not forgotten the ruin that came to you in Cincinnati. You certainly would not dare to go back to the city again." "But mother," replied the daughter in tears, "there are thousands of poor girls there who are what I was. The Lord has saved me and called me to go back and bring them to Him. My own salvation depends upon earnest work for their salvation. I love you and father dearly; I regret to leave the good home you have given me, but I must go back and down to serve in the slums to rescue the perishing."

And she did go back. For years she labored most successfully among the fallen girls of the city; she led scores and hundreds to Christ. I heard her give her witness and preach a wonderful sermon of redeeming grace after long years of service when the gray hairs were mingling with the gold. For many years she had lived in the very depths of sin, blessedly kept from the stain of sin. She had gone into the dens of vice untouched by vice. She had gone down into the stench of the slums unpolluted by the crime and sins of the slums, and carrying with her the fragrance and sweetness of the holiness of heart and righteousness of life which have been brought to us through the sufferings of our blessed Lord.

This was the mission of Jesus on earth—to take us out of the world, to take the world out of us, and then to send us back into the world to live and labor, kept by the power of the indwelling Holy Spirit, untainted by the sins and the sinners among whom we move and witness, love, pray and labor for. Jesus came to redeem a people and keep them here and use them in the salvation of other people. There ought not to be one of us who has been saved and who is walking with our Lord today, but of whom He can say, "They are not of the world, even as I am not of the world." Who, if we undertook to tell our religious experience in detail, would not tell of some one who was a witness to us of the power of Christ, who was solicitous for our salvation, who let their light so shine before us that we were led to give God glory for the gift of His Son.

When Jesus prays for the sanctification of His disciples He does not simply mean that they shall be set apart for service; there is a deeper and higher meaning to this. He wants them to be cleansed, to be made pure, and to be filled with the Holy Spirit in order that they may have power to render acceptable and fruitful service. He is seeking that they shall be fully prepared and equipped to fulfil the mission on which He is going to send them forth. He says, "As thou hast sent me into the world, even so have I also sent them into the world."

The Father sent the Son into the world to

live a holy life before it, to bear a holy witness to it, and to give Himself a holy sacrifice
for it.   And it is for this same purpose that
our Lord Jesus sent His disciples of old, and
has sent His disciples throughout the gener-
ations, and does send His disciples today to live
holy lives before the world, to give a holy witness to the world, and then give themselves a
holy sacrifice for the world.   May God grant
the writer of these lines, and all those who may
read them, the spirit of self-surrender, of true
consecration, and of a living, mighty faith
which will bring into us the spirit and power
of our Christ;   the abiding and enduement of
the Holy Ghost that will enable us to walk before our fellowbeings, give a testimony to our
fellowbeings, and give ourselves in zealous
service for the salvation of our fellowbeings
that will enable us in the end to come to our
Master with our arms full of sheaves.

www.ingramcontent.com/pod-product-compliance
Lightning Source LLC
Chambersburg PA
CBHW020040040426
42331CB00030B/115